# BABY KNITS

## Accessories

igloobooks

Published in 2015
by Igloo Books Ltd
Cottage Farm
Sywell
NN6 0BJ
www.igloobooks.com

Cover images © Thinkstock / Getty Images

LEO002 1015
2 4 6 8 10 9 7 5 3
ISBN 978-1-78440-326-3

Printed and manufactured in China

# BABY KNITS

## Accessories

# Contents

# Introduction

Knitting for babies is a particular favourite with knitters of all levels, not just because of the small and sweet designs, but because of the inherently personal quality that comes with a lovingly woven, hand-knit item. Baby knits are the perfect way to commemorate the arrival of a precious new-born, whether you're knitting for your own baby or for a family member or friend. Imagine receiving such an affectionately crafted gift for your child, to be worn and played with, and cherished for years to come. Baby knits are a joy to receive, a joy to knit and are highly rewarding little projects.

This book contains everything you need to create gorgeous, soft and truly special baby accessories. A helpful and detailed introduction provides an illustrated guide to basic stitches and essential knitting skills for beginners, to help you get started. There is also an adorable range of accessories to knit for babies. Each pattern is accompanied by beautiful photographs, alongside clear instructions and charts and diagrams where necessary. From vintage-inspired bonnets to cosy blankets, this is a lovely guide to knits for babies.

# Learn to knit:
# Knitting Essentials

Learning the lingo, understanding needle sizes and being able to change colours are essentials that every keen knitter should know.

Knitting is an enjoyable and rewarding hobby, but sometimes it can be daunting. It may look like a world of meaningless letters and confusing numbers but by learning the lingo and becoming familiar with the tools and techniques, it will all make sense. Knitting abbreviations are one of the trickiest elements of the knitting world, but 'k2tog' does actually mean something. The list opposite will decipher the code and it will soon be second nature.

Needles come in a wide variety of sizes. They are your most vital tool so it is important that you know your 6s from your 6mm. Thin needles are required for small and fine projects whereas larger needles are used for chunkier tasks.

The chart opposite will help you choose the right needle for your chosen project. We will also guide you through the basics of changing colour for when you are ready to move on.

## Needle Conversion Chart

| mm | UK | US |
|---|---|---|
| 2.0 mm | 14 | 0 |
| 2.25 mm | 13 | 1 |
| 2.5 mm | 12 | |
| 2.75 mm | 12 | 2 |
| 3.0 mm | 11 | 3 |
| 3.25 mm | 10 | 3 |
| 3.5 mm | 9 | 4 |
| 3.75 mm | 9 | 5 |
| 4.0 mm | 8 | 6 |
| 4.5 mm | 7 | 7 |
| 5.0 mm | 6 | 8 |
| 5.5 mm | 5 | 9 |
| 6.0 mm | 4 | 10 |
| 6.5 mm | 3 | 10½ |
| 7.0 mm | 2 | |
| 7.5 mm | 1 | |
| 8.0 mm | 0 | 11 |
| 9.0 mm | 00 | 13 |
| 10 mm | 000 | 15 |

## Changing Colour

Changing colour to create stripes is most easily done at the end of a row. First, knit all the rows that you need to, with your first colour.

When you are ready to change colour, drop the old colour. Pick up the new colour by threading the beginning of the new colour through the back of the last stitch and pulling the old colour tightly, trapping the new colour.

Hold both the start of the new colour and the end of the old colour together and resume knitting as normal, using the new colour. After every row, pull the end of the new colour to keep it tight, but ensure that the tension is kept even. Cut the old colour, leaving a 15cm/6in tail. Use a tapestry needle to weave the loose ends in.

## Abbreviations

| | | | | | | | |
|---|---|---|---|---|---|---|---|
| **alt** | alternate | **m1** | make one* | **sl1** | slip 1 st |
| **approx.** | approximately | **m1l** | make one left | **skpo** | sl1, k1, pass sl st over |
| **beg** | beginning | **m1r** | make one right | **sm** | slip marker |
| **CC** | contrast colour | **m1p** | make one purl | **ssk** | slip first st, slip second st, then knit both together off right-hand needle |
| **cont** | continue | **MC** | main colour | | |
| **dec** | decrease(ing) | **N1/N2** | needle 1/needle 2 | | |
| **DPN** | double-pointed needle | **p** | purl | **st(s)** | stitch(es) |
| **foll** | following | **p2tog** | purl 2 together | **st st** | stocking stitch |
| **folls** | follows | **patt** | pattern | **tbl** | through back loop |
| **g st** | garter stitch | **pm** | place marker | **tog** | together |
| **inc** | increase(ing) | **psso** | pass slipped st over | **w&t** | wrap and turn |
| **k** | knit | **pwise** | purlwise | **wyif** | with yarn in front |
| **k2tog** | knit 2 together | **rem** | remain(ing) | **WS** | wrong side |
| **kfb** | knit into front and back of stitch | **rep** | repeat | **yf** | yarn forward |
| **KTS** | knit the steek st | **rnd** | round | **yo** | yarn over |
| **kwise** | knitwise | **RH** | right hand | **yon** | yarn over needle |
| **LH** | left hand | **RS** | right side | **yrn** | yarn round needle |

*make one by lifting the bar between sts, placing it onto the LH needle and knitting into the back of the lifted bar

# Learn to knit:
# The Basic Stitches

The following pages contain the basic stitches that you will need to begin knitting. Each how-to section covers a different stitch, with comprehensive step-by-step explanation and accompanying images.

## Long-tail cast on

This uses a single needle and produces an elastic knitted edge like a row of garter stitch.

### Step 1

Leaving an end about three times the length of the required cast-on, put a slipknot on the needle. Holding the yarn end in the left hand, take the left thumb under the yarn and upwards. Insert the needle in the loop just made on the thumb.

### Step 2

Use the ball end of the yarn to make a knit stitch, slipping the loop off the thumb. Pull the yarn end to close the stitch up to the needle. Continue making stitches in this way.

## Chain cast off

A simple knit stitch cast off is used in most of these projects. Knit two stitches. * With the left needle, lift the first stitch over the second. Knit the next stitch. Repeat from * until one stitch remains. Break the yarn, take the end through this stitch and tighten.

### Slipknot

### Step 1

A slipknot is the first stage of any cast on. Loop the yarn around two fingers of the left hand, the ball end on top. Dip the needle into the loop, catch the ball end of the yarn and pull it through the loop.

### Step 2

Pull the ends of the yarn to tighten the knot. Tighten the ball end to bring the knot up to the needle.

### Ends

The end of yarn left after casting on should be a reasonable length; approx 10–30cm/4–12in, so that it can be used for sewing up. The same applies to the end left after casting off.

# Knit Stitch (K)

Choose to hold the yarn and needles in whichever way you feel most comfortable. To create tension in the yarn – that is, to keep it moving evenly – you will need to twist it through some fingers of the hand holding the yarn, and maybe even take it around your little finger. Continuous rows of knit stitch produce garter stitch. It does take some practice to get the stitches even so don't be discouraged, keep on practising.

**Step 1**

Insert the right needle into the first stitch on the left needle. Make sure it goes from left to right into the front of the stitch.

**Step 2**

Taking the yarn behind, bring it up and around the right needle.

**Step 3**

Using the tip of the right needle, draw a loop of yarn through the stitch.

**Step 4**

Slip the stitch off the left needle. There is now a new stitch on the right needle.

# Purl Stitch (P)

**Step 1**

Insert the right needle into the first stitch on the left needle. Make sure it goes into the stitch from right to left.

**Step 2**

Lower the tip of the right needle, taking it away from you to draw a loop of yarn through the stitch.

**Step 3**

Taking the yarn to the front, loop it around the right needle.

**Step 4**

Slip the stitch off the left needle. There is now a new stitch on the right needle.

# Decreases

Decreases have two basic functions. They can be used to reduce the number of stitches in a row, as in armholes and necklines, and combined with increases, they can create stitch patterns.

## Right slanting single decreases (k2tog)

Knitting two stitches together makes a smooth shaping, with the second stitch lying on top of the first.

### Step 1

Insert the right needle through the front of the first two stitches on the left needle, then take the yarn around the needle.

### Step 2

Draw the loop through and drop the two stitches off the left needle.

## Left slanting double decreases (sk2po)

For a double decrease that slants to the left, worked on a right-side row, you'll need to take the first stitch over a single decrease. For a similar-looking decrease worked on a wrong-side row, purl three together through the back of the loops (p3tog tbl).

### Step 1

Insert the right needle knitwise through the front of the first stitch on the left needle, and slip it onto the right needle.

### Step 2

Knit the next two stitches together, then lift the first stitch over as shown. To make a right-slanting double decrease, simply knit three stitches together (k3tog).

# Yarn Over (yo)

It's essential to take the yarn over the needle so that the strand lies in the same direction as the other stitches. Working into this strand on the next row makes a hole, but if the strand is twisted, the hole will close up.

When the stitch before a yarn over is purl, the yarn will already be at the front, ready to go over the needle.

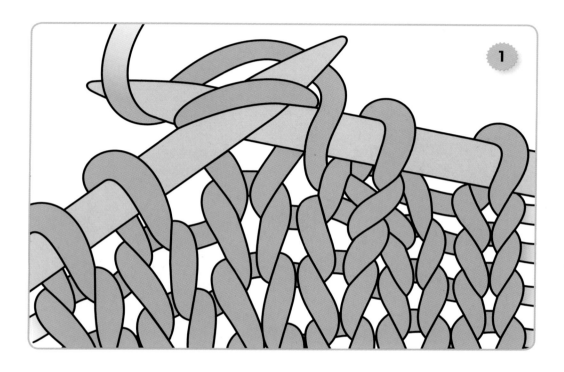

### Step 1

To make a yarn over between knit stitches, bring the yarn to the front as if to purl, then take it over the needle to knit the next stitch.

### Step 2

To make a yarn over between a knit and a purl, bring the yarn to the front as if to purl, take it over the needle and bring it to the front again, ready to purl.

# Increases

Here are two of the most basic methods of increasing a single stitch – bar increase and lifted strand increase.

## Bar increase on a knit row (kfb)

Knitting into the front and the back of a stitch is the most common increase. It's a neat, firm increase, which makes a little bar on the right side of the work at the base of the new stitch. This makes it easy to count rows between shapings and doesn't leave a hole.

### Step 1

Knit into the front of the stitch and pull the loop through, but leave the stitch on the left needle.

### Step 2

Knit into the back of the stitch on the left needle.

### Step 3

Slip the stitch off the left needle, making two stitches on the right needle. Note that the bar of the new stitch lies on the left.

## Lifted strand increase to the left (ml or mlL)

Making a stitch from the strand between stitches is a very neat way to increase.

### Picture A

From the front, insert the left needle under the strand between stitches. Make sure the strand lies on the needle in the same direction as the other stitches, then knit into the back of it.

## Lifted strand increase to the right (mlR)

This right-slanting increase balances exactly the lifted strand increase to the left.

### Picture B

From the back, insert the left needle under the strand between the stitches. It will not lie in the same direction as the other stitches, so knit into the front of it.

## Double increase

This is one of the simplest ways to make three stitches out of one.

### Picture C

Knit one stitch without slipping it off, take the yarn over the right needle from front to back then knit the same stitch again. A small but decorative hole is left in the fabric.

# Twists

Twisting stitches is working two or three stitches out of sequence, but without using a cable needle.
This is an easy way to create patterns where lines of stitches travel over the surface of the knitting.

## Left twist (t2L)

This twist is worked on a right-side row. As the stitches change place, the first stitch lies on top and slants
to the left, while the stitch behind is worked through the back of the loop.

**Step 1**

Knit into the back of the
second stitch.

**Step 2**

Knit into the front of the first stitch.

**Step 3**

Slip both stitches off the left
needle together.

## Right twist (t2R)

In this right-sided row twist, the second stitch lies on top and slants to the right, while the stitch behind is worked
through the back of the loop.

**Step 1**

Knit into the front of the
second stitch.

**Step 2**

Knit into the back of first stitch.

**Step 3**

Slip both stitches off the left
needle together.

# Learn to knit:
# Fair Isle

Fair Isle or stranded knitting is a really popular technique and it's easy when you know how.

Traditional Fair Isle may use many colours in the design. However, only two colours are typically used in a row, which makes it less complex to work than it seems. Patterns are worked in stocking stitch from charts, using colours or symbols to indicate each different colour. Charts are read from the bottom, starting at the right-hand side. Each square represents a stitch, each row of squares a row of knitting.

In flat knitting, right side rows are normally worked from right to left, wrong side rows from left to right. Odd numbered rows will usually be knit, even rows purl. In circular knitting, all rows are read from right to left and, as a rule with Fair Isle, all rows will be knit as the right side of the work is always facing you.

## Yarn

For good pattern definition, a fine Shetland wool is traditionally used, being warm, light and durable. Other wool will work well and Fair Isle patterns can be found on a wide range of projects from fine socks through to heavier sweaters and jackets.

Try swatching non-wool yarns for handle and appearance. Some yarns, especially cottons, can be slippery, which can make maintaining even tension more difficult.

## Colour changing

When changing colours, the yarn not in use (the 'float' or 'float yarn') is carried across the wrong side of the work by stranding or weaving in to avoid constantly breaking off and rejoining the yarn.

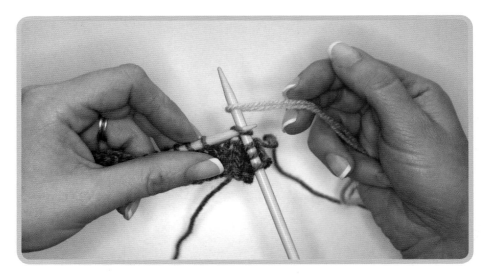

**Knit row**

1. To work the chart shown, starting at the bottom right and working from right to left, knit in colour A (dark blue) until the first colour change. Make the next stitch by joining in colour B (light blue) as normal. Leave a tail of B for darning in later and don't cut off A.

2. Knit in B to the next colour change. Lift yarn A from beneath, under B, and knit with A until the next colour change. Repeat for each colour change, lifting the new yarn from under the working yarn.

Repeat this process, changing yarn according to the chart until the end of the row. At the end of the row check that when the fabric is slightly stretched, the floats are not pulling the fabric in.

## Stranding

This method works well where colour changes are frequent (no more than four or five stitches apart). It gives a less dense, lighter fabric and uses less yarn than weaving in.

## Weaving in

Weaving in avoids loose floats across the back of the work and the two colours in the row are neatly entwined together at each stitch.

Both techniques have their place. Stranding is ideal for areas with frequent colour changes within the row and where a lighter, less dense fabric is required.

For firmer fabrics, where the floats would be too long or where even short floats would be likely to snag, weaving in may be preferable. With socks or gloves, the floats may catch on rings or between toes. This can be annoying and may spoil your knitting so weaving in may be the better method here for changing colours within the row.

**Purl row**

1. Work the next row of the chart from right to left in purl. As with the knit row, lift the new colour from beneath the working yarn at each colour change so the old yarn lies in front of the new yarn as it faces you.

**Weaving in: Knit Row, using B.**

1. To work a stitch in yarn B (light blue), A (dark blue) is woven in. Insert RH needle to begin a k st as normal. Take A over the top of B and wrap round RH needle as if to knit. Take B around RH needle as if to k. A sits behind B on RH needle.

2. Before completing the k st, bring A back around the RH needle. Note how A now lies over B. Leaving A over B, k the next st as normal in B.

### Semi-stranding or catching in

Sometimes there's a long run of stitches in a single colour. In this case, it's possible to catch in the second colour every three or four stitches using the weaving-in method (left). This differs from the full weaving-in technique because the yarn is only woven in every few stitches rather than every single stitch. This technique may combine better with stranding as it's less dense and better matches the feel and density of a stranded fabric.

The best way to decide which method to use is by swatching. Test each section of the pattern, bearing in mind the type of garment or accessory you're making. Where will the pattern be? Will it get lots of wear? Is it likely to be in an area prone to snagging?

**Can the techniques be combined?**
Yes – in fact, it may be unavoidable with some patterns, but you need to swatch carefully.

With properly worked swatches, there should not be any difference in the tension, but be aware of the feel of the fabric. Be sure to include some rows of single-colour knitting in your swatches if they feature in the pattern as these may also feel slightly different to the coloured sections.

# Learn to knit:
# Double Knitting

Many of us love colourwork but are frustrated by the messy wrong side – this clever technique creates a completely reversible fabric.

Double knitting is a fascinating technique that can be used in a variety of ways. This section looks at using double knitting to create reversible, double-faced fabric where both sides of the fabric are interlocked and joined together.

This kind of double knitting can be worked flat or in the round and colourwork looks stunning. With double knitting, a red star on a white background on one side magically transforms into a white star on a red background when viewed from the other side, and no one will know how you did it!

## How double knitting works

While there's no problem simply following the instructions and accepting that the pattern does what it says on the tin, you may find it helpful when following charts to understand how the technique works. A knit stitch is smooth on the side facing you and has a bump on the reverse. Purl stitches on the other hand show a bump on the front as they face you but are smooth on the side facing away from you.

The nature of this knitting technique means that the bumps are trapped between the smooth knit stitches and therefore can't be seen. This leaves only the smooth (right) sides visible on both outer faces of the fabric.

## Terminology

As both sides of the work are effectively the right side, you may find it easier to think of the two sides as A and B. Each yarn will be both main (background) and contrasting (foreground) yarn, so if yarn X is the main colour (MC) on side A, it will be the contrasting colour (CC) on side B.

Yarn Y will then be the CC on side A but the MC on side B. The colours may also be referred to in patterns as MC1 and MC2.

## Casting on

Double knitting patterns normally specify a cast on. If not, you can use any cast on, working with both yarns at the same time. Note that you will cast on twice as many stitches as there are squares in your chart as each square represents two stitches.

Before you begin knitting, make sure that the stitches are in pairs in the same order – for example, all the pairs should be XY. Using both colours will create a two-colour cast-on edge. For a single colour edge, a provisional cast on such as tubular cast on can be used.

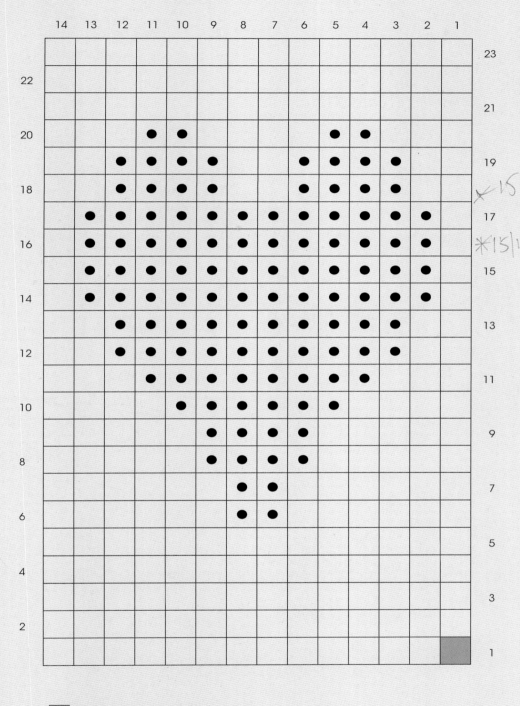

## Reading double knitting charts

Double knitting patterns are usually charted. Unlike in regular knitting, in double knitting each square on the chart represents two stitches.

Depending on the colour of the square, this will determine which colour yarn is knitted and which yarn is purled.

As the two fabrics form a reversible pattern, a stitch knitted on side A in yarn X will give a visible stitch in X on side A. If a stitch is purled using yarn X on side A, this stitch will not be seen on side A but will be visible on side B.

As with other charts, charts for flat knitting read right to left then left to right. For knitting in the round, all rows read right to left.

■ Start knitting here

☐ Odd rows (side A knit in X (MC1), purl in Y (MC2))
Even rows (side B knit in Y (MC2), purl in X (MC1))

• Odd rows (side A knit in Y (MC1), purl in X (MC2))
Even rows (side B knit in X (MC1), purl in Y (MC2))

## Flat & circular knitting

## Step 1

Below the contrasting yarn you will see a series of bumps made in the main yarn (X).

These bumps are picked up in this row, increasing the stitches and forming the stitches for one face of the fabric (side A). The existing stitches form the other face (B).

## Need to know

### Tubular cast on

Using a piece of smooth contrasting waste yarn, cast on half the total number of stitches needed plus one extra stitch (You can use the backwards loop method as this is easier to unpick later).

For our sample chart (see page 15), cast on 15 stitches (total stitches = 28, halved = 14, plus 1 = 15).

### Set up rows

**Knitting in the round**

Join work into circle and check that there are no twisted stitches.

Change to yarn X.

**Set Up Row 1:** P2, p2tog, p to end.

**Set Up Row 2:** Purl.

Change to yarn Y.

**Set Up Row 3:** Purl.

**Set Up Row 4:** Purl. Purl side should be facing you.

### Flat knitting

Change to yarn X.

**Set Up Row 1:** P2, p2tog, p to end.

**Set Up Row 2:** Knit.

Change to yarn Y.

**Set Up Row 3:** Purl.

**Set Up Row 4:** Knit. Purl side should be facing you.

## Step 2

**Chart Row 1 (Side A):** *With RH needle, lift bump of main yarn (X) below contrasting yarn, place on LH needle and ktbl. Bring both yarns X (MC1) and Y (MC2) to front of work and p next stitch using just yarn Y. Repeat from * to last stitch.

## Step 3

Check you have the correct number of stitches before proceeding. The final stitch should be a purl to maintain the pairing of stitches. For flat knitting, turn to work side B (chart row 2). For knitting in the round, place a marker and continue knitting round 2 (chart row 2) without turning the work. Note that you will have twice the number of stitches as squares shown in the chart (28 sts, 14 squares on the chart). This is because each square represents two stitches. The waste yarn can be carefully removed after several rows have been worked.

## Flat knitting

## Step 4

Hold both yarns to the back of the work, but knit the next stitch in just yarn Y.

## Step 5

Bring both yarns to front of work. Keeping both yarns at the front, but using yarn X (MC1) only, purl next stitch. The first chart square is now completed.

## Finishing a row (flat knitting only)

When working flat/straight (as opposed to knitting in the round), you will need to make a neat finish to the edges. For a tidy edge with a neat, solid line of each colour running up the sides, try the following technique:

## Step 6

Repeat steps 4 and 5 to last square on chart. Two stitches on LH needle. Keeping both yarns at back of work, slip next stitch purlwise (as if to purl).

## Step 7

Bring yarn that is the same colour as the final stitch (X in this case), to the front of work. (One yarn either side of work). Keeping just this one yarn to the front, slip final stitch purlwise.

The side facing you (B) will have a row of smooth stitches in colour Y (MC2), the side facing away from you (A) will have a row of smooth stitches in colour X (MC1). Purl stitches worked in X (MC1) produce a barely visible bump on side B facing you but are visible and smooth when viewed on side A.

## Step 8

Turn the work. One yarn (Y in this case) is in front, facing you and one is at the back, away from you (X). Knit first stitch in the same colour as the final stitch of the last row (X in this case).

## Step 9

Bring X (MC1) to the front. Both yarns are now together at the front of the work. Purl next stitch with just yarn Y (MC2).

## Step 10

Take both yarns to back and continue to work rest of row, knitting in X (MC1), purling in Y (MC2). By working in this way at the end of each row, after several rows you will see a neat row of chain stitches up each side of the work.

## Knitting in the round

Repeat steps 4 and 5 following chart (see page 15), but, because you are always working with side A facing you, work knit stitches in X (MC1) and purls in Y (MC2), still with two stitches for each square on chart. Mark end of round with a stitch marker.

The side facing you (A) will have a row of smooth stitches in colour X (MC1), the side facing away from you (B) will have a row of smooth stitches in colour Y (MC2). Purl stitches worked in Y (MC2) produce a barely visible bump on side A facing you but are visible and smooth when viewed on side B.

## Step 11

The next pair of stitches need to produce a visible stitch in CC (Y on this row). To produce a visible stitch we need to knit it, so if we want a visible stitch in Y we have to knit the next stitch in Y.

## Step 12

We don't want to see the next stitch on this side of the work so it is purled using X.

## Step 13

Repeat this process for each CC square on the chart. When a square is shown in MC, work these stitches by knitting in X and purling in Y. Note that we are still working knit, purl, but we will have two same-colour stitches next to one another at each colour change.

## Need to know

### Working patterns and motifs

When you reach the first pattern row for the motif, it helps if you think in terms of main colour (MC) and contrast colour (CC). Unlike other colourwork, there are no solid runs of a single colour since every chart square is worked twice and every square will always be worked once in each colour. What changes is not the order of knit and purl (this always stays the same) but which colour of the pair you use to knit with and which colour you purl with.

Looking at Row 6 in our chart, whether you are working flat or in the round, the motif begins with side A facing you. The knit stitches on this side (A) were worked in yarn X, so X is our MC for this face of the work. Yarn Y is therefore the CC. Work as above, working the knit stitches in X and purling the paired stitches in Y until you reach the colour change.

## Casting off

## Step 14

For a neat cast off, grafting (kitchener stitch) is a great choice. For this, you will need two double-pointed needles (DPNs) in the same size as your main knitting. Work to within one row of the end of the pattern. Holding 2 DPNs parallel in your RH, slip knit stitches onto front needle and purl stitches onto back needle. To avoid a stepped finish, work one row of purl on just the stitches on the back needle. Don't turn the work but slide the knitting back to the RH end of the DPNs. Graft the two edges together as normal. Whereas on side B the heart is in yarn X with the background in Y, when viewed from side A, the heart is in yarn Y with the background in X.

**Need to know**

### Flat knitting

At the end of the row, follow the steps for finishing a row as above, then work side B. As side B has Y as the MC, X is the CC, so work all MC squares with the knit stitch in Y and the purl stitch in X. Work CC squares with X as the knit stitch and Y as the purl stitch.

**Note:** Remember that in flat knitting, rows on a chart are worked right to left then left to right.

### Knitting in the round

When knitting projects in the round, there will be no edge stitches so no need to perform any slipped stitch manoeuvres at the end of the round and you can ignore the section for finishing a row (above).

Charts for knitting in the round are always worked from right to left so you will always have side A facing you. This makes things easier as the MC and CC will remain the same throughout.

# Learn to knit:
# Cable Knitting

Knitting groups of stitches out of sequence creates exciting stitch patterns. Cables can be worked with two or more stitches and crossed to the front or the back.

For rich texture and dramatic shape it is impossible to ignore cables. In their simplest terms, cables are essentially combinations of knit and purl stitches worked out of sequence.

Cables can be worked in an endless variety of sizes and combinations. Stitches are transferred to a short needle (a cable needle) and these stitches are then held either at the front or the back of the knitting.

A number of stitches are then knitted from the main needle. To complete the sequence, the stitches from the cable needle are then knitted.

This has the effect of creating a crossed fabric. Where stitches are held at the back the cross will be to the right. Stitches held at the front will create a cross moving to the left.

## What are cables?

Cables are usually worked in knit stitches on a reverse stocking stitch background.

The contrast between the smooth knit stitches and the bumpy, dense purl side of the reverse stocking stitch allows the cable pattern to stand out clearly.

Cables can be simple, single braids or complex combinations of braids, honeycombs and plaits.

## Hints & tips

Cable needles come in straight versions, straight with a kink in the middle or occasionally hooked which can prevent stitches sliding off. Choose whichever works best for you If you don't have a cable needle handy, use a short DPN.

## Step 1

For a simple six-stitch cable that crosses to the left, purl to where the cable begins. Take a cable needle in the same (or slightly smaller) size as the main needles. Hold it in the RH, slightly above and parallel to the RH needle. Slip the next three stitches onto the cable needle as if you were going to purl them (p-wise).

## Step 2

Slide the slipped stitches (these will be worked later) along to the centre of the cable needle and hold the cable needle with stitches on to the front of the work. The cable needle can be supported in the RH as you work the next stitches or left loose at the front of the work. Alternatively, you can carefully poke it into the fabric but care should be taken not to split the yarn or snag the fabric.

## Step 3

Knit the next three stitches from LH main needle as normal. Avoid a hole at the crossover point by drawing up the yarn quite firmly after the first stitch. These stitches may feel tight and quite difficult to work. Don't worry, this is normal!

## Step 4

Next, work the stitches on the cable needle. Leave LH main needle at back of work. With cable needle in LH in front of the LH main needle, slide the stitches to the RH end of the cable needle. Be careful to keep the stitches in the same order and make sure you don't twist the stitches when lifting the needle.

## Step 5

This completes the LH-twisted cable. This type of cable may also be referred to in some patterns as a left cross, LH or front-cross cable.

## Step 6

For a cable that twists to the right, purl up to the point where the cable is to be made. Slip the next three stitches onto a cable needle. This time, hold the cable needle to the back of the work. Again, if it is easier, poke the needle through the knitted fabric, but being careful to avoid 'pulls'.

## Step 7

Knit the next three stitches from the LH main needle.

## Step 8

Now bring the cable needle to the front of the work, taking the LH main needle to the back. Be careful not to twist the stitches. Knit the three stitches from the cable needle in their original order.

## Step 9

This completes the right-twist cable (also referred to as a right cross, RH or back-cross cable). Depending on the pattern a number of 'plain' rows (rows with just knit and purl and no cabled or crossed stitches) may now be worked before the next cable row.

**Step 10**

In this swatch a left-twist cable is combined with a right-twist cable to create a wave effect. Two cables are also worked at either end of the swatch. Each cable is separated by purl stitches and a purl band is worked at each edge to make the cables stand out. There is lots of fun to be had playing with cable combinations.

# Accessories

Here are some adorable little accessories for your beloved babies. They're quick to make, so they make ideal last-minute gifts.

# Elfine Hood

**1**
Beginner

This simple hood was inspired by the designer's love of vintage knitting patterns, but it looks as good today as it would've done fifty years ago.

Most of us love knitting for babies and children, but it can be frustrating when they grow out of their lovingly knitted gifts so soon. The beauty of a hood like this is that it will last a little while longer than a jumper or a pair of booties, so you'll get the maximum out of this gorgeous yarn.

## Border

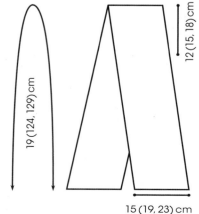

CAST ON

Cast on 30 (37, 44) sts.

**Row 1 (WS):** P 0(1,0), *k1tbl, p1; rep from * to end.

**Row 2:** Knit.

**Row 3:** K 0(1,0) tbl, *p1, k1tbl; rep from * to end.

**Row 4:** Knit.

Rep these four rows once more, then rep Row 1.

## Body

**Row 1 (RS):** K9 (9, 9), *k3, yo, k2tog, k2; rep from * to end.

**Row 2:** [P3, yo, p2tog, p2] 3 (4, 5) times, [p1, k1tbl] 4 times, p1.

**Row 3:** As for Row 1 of body section.

**Row 4:** [P3, yo, p2tog, p2] 3 (4, 5) times, [k1tbl, p1] 4 times, k1tbl.

Rep these four rows until work measures 96 (121, 126) cm from cast on edge, ending with Row 3.

## Border

**Row 1:** K 0(1,0) tbl, *p1, k1tbl; rep from * to end.

**Row 2:** Knit.

**Row 3:** P 0(1,0), *k1tbl, p1; rep from * to end.

**Row 4:** Knit.

Rep these four rows once more, then rep Row 1.

Cast off.

**Finishing:** Fold scarf in half lengthways with WS together. Make hood by joining back edges together and using mattress stitch form a seam 12 (15, 18) cm long from fold. Wash and block.

## Schematic

119 (124, 129) cm

12 (15, 18) cm

15 (19, 23) cm

## About this pattern

### Sizing
Baby (Toddler, Child)

### Yarn
Lion Brand Superwash Merino Cashmere – 2 (3, 4) x 40g balls in Blossom

### About the yarn
Aran weight; 80m per 40g; 72% Superwash Merino wool, 15% nylon, 13% cashmere

### Needles
5mm straight

### Tension
Measured St st:

10 cm

10 cm

24 rows

20 sts

### Other supplies
Tapestry needle

# Darling Bonnet & Booties

**2**
Intermediate

This pretty little set makes a great gift for newborns and you only need one ball for the whole set!

## About this pattern

### Sizing

Newborn (6 months, 12 months)
To fit head 30 (35, 40) cm
To fit foot length 7 (8, 10) cm

### Yarn

Betty and Belle DK
1 ball each in Vanilla Slice

### About the yarn

DK; 75m per 25g ball; 100% acrylic

### Needles

4mm straight

### Tension

Measured over St st:

10 cm

10 cm

28 rows

24 sts

### Other supplies

50cm of 6mm ribbon for bonnet
80cm of 3mm ribbon for booties
Stitch holder
Tapestry needle

---

It's surprising how much further your yarn goes when you're knitting a lace pattern and this design is proof of that. Note that our little model is accidentally wearing the bonnet backwards (whoops!) but hopefully you'll still get a good idea of how it should look.

## Bonnet

**CAST ON**

Cast on 54 (60, 66) sts.

Knit 11 rows.

**Next row (inc row):** K6, p8 (11, 11), [pfb] 25 (25, 31) times, p9 (12, 12), k6. 79 (85, 97) sts.

**Begin Lace pattern:**

**Row 1 (RS):** K7, *yo, ssk, k1, k2tog, yo, k1; rep from * to last 6 sts, k6.

**Row 2 and even rows:** K6, p to last 6 sts, k6.

**Row 3:** K7, *k1, yo, sk2po, yo, k2; rep from * to last 6 sts, k6.

**Row 5:** K7, *k2tog, yo, k1, yo, ssk, k1; rep from * to last 6 sts, k6.

**Row 7:** K6, k2tog, yo, *k3, yo, sk2po, yo; rep from * to last 11 sts, k3, yo, ssk, k6.

**Row 8:** As for Row 2.

These 8 rows form patt.

Cont in patt until work measures 10 (11, 12) cm from beg of lace patt, ending with Row 1 or 5.

## Shape crown:

**Row 1 (WS):** K6, p to last 12 sts and turn.

**Row 2 (RS):** Sl1, patt to last 12 sts and turn.

**Row 3:** Sl1, p to last 18 sts and turn.

**Row 4:** Sl1, patt to last 18 sts and turn.

**Row 5:** Sl1, p to last 24 sts and turn.

**Row 6:** Sl1, patt to last 24 sts and turn.

**Row 7:** Sl1, p to end. 79 (85, 97) sts.

**Dec row:** K10 (7, 9), *sk2po, k1; rep from * to last 9 (6, 8) sts, k to end. 49 (49, 57) sts.

Knit 1 row.

### 12m size only:

Dec row: K6, k2tog, k8, *k3tog, k8; rep from * to last 8 sts, k2tog, k6. 49 sts.

Knit 1 row.

### All sizes:

Dec row 1: K6, k2tog, k6, *k3tog, k6; rep from * to last 8 sts, k2tog, k6. 41 sts.

Knit 1 row.

Dec row 2: K6, k2tog, k4, *k3tog, k4; rep from * to last 8 sts, k2tog, k6. 33 sts.

Knit 1 row.

Dec row 3: K6, k2tog, k2, *k3tog, k2; rep from * to last 8 sts, k2tog, k6. 25 sts.

Knit 1 row.

Dec row 4: K6, k2tog, *k3tog; rep from * to last 8 sts, k2tog, k6. 17 sts.

Knit 1 row.

Dec row 5: K5, k2tog, k3tog, k2tog, k5. 13 sts.

Dec row 6: K5, k2tog, k6. 12 sts.

Cast off.

Fold cast-off sts in half and sew to create back seam.

Cut ribbon in half and attach at each side of neck.

**Finishing:** Block gently by steaming bonnet to shape, without allowing the iron to touch the fabric.

## Booties

Cast on 25 (31, 37) sts.

Knit 2 rows.

**Begin Lace patt:**

**Row 1 (RS):** K1, *yo, ssk, k1, k2tog, yo, k1; rep from * to end.

**Row 2 and even rows:** Purl.

**Row 3:** K1, *k1, yo, sk2po, yo, k2; rep from * to end.

**Row 5:** K1, *k2tog, yo, k1, yo, ssk, k1; rep from * to end.

**Row 7:** K2tog, yo, *k3, yo, sk2po, yo; rep from * to last 5 sts, k3, yo, ssk.

**Row 8:** As for Row 2.

These 8 rows form patt.

Work 8 (8, 12) more rows in patt.

**NEWBORN SIZE ONLY:**

Knit to last 2 sts, M1, knit to end. 26 sts.

22 (24, 26) cm

22.5 (25, 27.5) cm

10 (13, 15) cm

7 (8, 10) cm

## 6M AND 12M SIZES ONLY:

Knit to last 2 sts, k2tog. 30 (36) sts.

Purl 1 row.

Eyelet row: K2, *yo, k2tog, rep from * to last 2 sts, k2.

Purl 1 row.

### Shape instep:

**Next row:** K18 (20, 24), turn.

Leave foll 8 (10, 12) sts on holder.

**Next row:** P10 (10, 12), turn. Leave foll 8 (10, 12) sts on holder.

Working on the 10 (10, 12) sts on the needles only, work 12 (14, 16) rows in St st. Break off yarn.

With RS facing, rejoin yarn to first stitch holder on RH side of instep and k8 (10, 12), pu and k9 (11, 13) sts up side edge of instep, k10 (10, 12) sts from instep, pu and k9 (11, 13) sts evenly down side edge of instep and k8 (10, 12) sts from second stitch holder. 44 (52, 62) sts.

Knit 11 (13, 15) rows.

### Shape foot:

Dec row 1: K1, k2tog, k14 (18, 23), k2tog, k6, k2tog, k14 (18, 23), k2tog, k1. 40 (48, 58) sts.

Knit 1 row.

Dec row 2: K1, k2tog, k13 (17, 22), k2tog, k4, k2tog, k13 (17, 22), k2tog, k1. 36 (44, 54) sts.

Knit 1 row.

**Dec row 3:** K1, k2tog, k12 (16, 21), k2tog, k2, k2tog, k12 (16, 21), k2tog, k1. 32 (40, 50) sts.

Knit 1 row.

### 6M AND 12M SIZES ONLY:

**Dec row 4:** K1, k2tog, k(15, 20), [k2tog] twice, k(15, 20), k2tog, k1. 36 (46) sts. Knit 1 row.

### ALL SIZES:

Cast off.

Join leg and foot seam.

Cut ribbon in half and thread through eyelet row, tie in a bow at front of bootie.

| Symbol | Description |
|---|---|
| ☐ | RS: Knit / WS: Purl |
| ◯ | Yo |
| ╲ | RS: ssk / WS: p2tog tbl |
| ⋀ | RS: sl1, k2tog, psso / WS: sl1 wyit, p2tog tbl psso |
| ╱ | RS: k2tog / WS: p2tog |
| ☐ | Repeat |

# Stippling Blanket

Now you've learned how to do double knitting, practise your skills with this snuggly baby blanket.

**2**

Intermediate

This blanket makes use of the double layer created in double knitting to produce a super soft, snuggly blanket that babies will love – and so will parents, since the yarn is machine washable! You will be beginning with 632 stitches. This will probably require using all three circular needles at once. As you gradually reduce the number of stitches on the needles, you can use fewer circular needles, and eventually use a single circular needle, switching to the smaller-length circulars as you continue to decrease stitches. Switch to DPNs once the stitches will no longer fit on the smallest circular.

**CAST ON**

Loosely cast on 632 sts using the double knitting cast-on (see Special Instructions box), starting with a stitch of MC2 (ie MC1 on your thumb during the cast on). Join to work in the rnd, being careful not to twist. pm to mark beg of rnd.

**Set-up Rnd:** *K1 MC2 wyib, p1 MC1 wyif; rep from * to end.

**Rnd 1:** Sm, [work Row 1 of Chart A, pm] three times, work Row 1 of Chart A.

**Rnd 2 and all even rnds:** Sm, sl1 p-wise wyib, sl1 p-wise wyif, [work next row of Chart A as set] four times. 616 sts.

**Rnd 3 and all odd rnds:** [Sm, work next row of Chart A as set] four times.

Cont patt as set until all 25 rows of Chart A have been worked. 440 sts.

**Rnd 26:** Sm, sl1 p-wise wyib, sl1 p-wise wyif, [work Row 1 of Chart B] four times. 424 sts.

**Rnd 27 and all odd rnds:** [Sm, work next row of Chart B as set] four times.

**Rnd 28 and all even rnds:** Sm, sl1 p-wise wyib, sl1 p-wise wyif, [work next row of Chart B as set] four times. 408 sts.

Cont patt as set until all 53 rows of Chart B have been worked. 8 sts.

Break yarns.

Removing markers as you come to them, thread the tail of MC2 through the rem four MC2 stitches; and then thread the tail of MC1 through the remaining four MC1 stitches.

Weave in all ends as invisibly as possible between the two layers of the blanket.

## About this pattern

### Yarn

Crystal Palace Mochi Plus/ Solid 4 balls each in Intense Rainbow 551 (MC) and Ecru 1500 (CC)

**Note:** the sample uses very close to 200g of each yarn, you may like to buy 5 balls to be on the safe side.

### About the yarn

Aran; 87m per 50g ball; 80% Merino wool, 20% nylon

### Needles

6mm circular, 150cm
6mm circular, 80cm
6mm circular, 40cm
6mm DPNs

### Tension

Measured over double knitted St st:

10 cm

10 cm

22 rows

26 sts (13 per side)

### Other supplies

3 stitch markers
1 round marker (noticeably different from the stitch markers)
Cable needle

## Special instructions

This blanket uses a slightly different cast-on to the one recommended.

We've put step-by-step instructions from Kathleen on our website www.knitnowmag.co.uk

Reading charts: All chart rows should be read from right to left.

Cdd: (Sl st onto CN and hold in front, sl1 p-wise) twice, rm, sl st onto CN and hold in front, transfer 2 sts from RH needle back to LH needle, transfer 3 sts from CN back to LH

needle, wyib sl2 as if to k2tog, k1 MC2, pass slipped sts over, wyif sl2 as if to p2tog-tbl, p1 MC1, pass slipped sts over, pm.

## Chart A

## Schematic

67 cm

67 cm

## Chart B

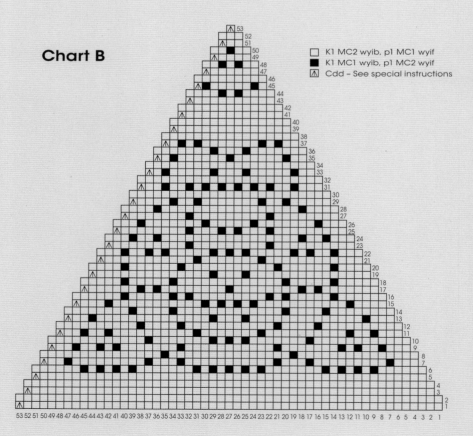

☐ K1 MC2 wyib, p1 MC1 wyif
■ K1 MC1 wyib, p1 MC2 wyif
⚠ Cdd – See special instructions

44

# Corner to Corner Blanket

This cute blanket is an easy introduction to lace and it's perfect for using up odds and ends of yarn.

## About this pattern

### Yarn
1 ball each in Blueberry Muffin, Peppermint Green, Strawberry Fool, 3 balls in Vanilla Slice

It's always good to have a lovely snuggly blanket to hand for baby. This one is fun to knit and easily adaptable to whatever yarn you have available, so feel free to experiment and try out different yarn.

### Needles
4mm straight

### Tension
Measured over St st

### Starting corner

**CAST ON**

With red yarn, cast on 3 sts.

**Row 1 (RS):** Knit.

**Row 2 and all WS rows:** K1, p to last st, k1.

**Row 3:** K1, yo, k1, yo, k1.

**Row 5:** K1, yo, k3, yo, k1.

**Row 6:** K1, p to last st, k1.

### Main body

Still using red, work Rows 1–8 of Inc Lace Pattern seven times.

Change to cream and work Rows 1–8 of Inc Lace Pattern six times.

Change to blue and work Rows 1–8 of Inc Lace Pattern four times.

Change to cream and work Rows 1–8 of Inc Lace Pattern twice.

Still using cream, work Rows 1–8 of Dec Lace Pattern twice.

Change to green and work Rows 1–8 of Dec Lace Pattern four times.

Change to cream and work Rows 1–8 of Dec Lace Pattern six times.

Change to red and work Rows 1–8 of Dec Lace Pattern seven times.

### Ending corner

Cont in red.

**Row 1:** K1, yo, sssk, k1, p1, yo, sk2p, yo, p1, k1, k3tog, yo, k1.

**Row 2 and all WS rows:** K1, p to last st, k1.

**Row 3:** K1, yo, sssk, p1, yo, sk2p, yo, p1, k3tog, yo, k1.

**Row 5:** K1, yo, sssk, yo, sk2p, yo, k3tog, yo, k1.

**Row 7:** K1, yo, sssk, k1, k3tog, yo, k1.

**Row 9:** K1, yo, sk2p, yo, k1.

**Row 11:** K3.

Cast off.

### Other supplies
Darning needle

### Hints & tips
If you're using the charts, please note that only RS rows are shown and they are read from right to left. For the WS rows, on every row you should work as follows:
**k1, p to last st, k1**

## Inc Lace Pattern

| 15 | 14 | 13 | 12 | 11 | 10 | 9 | 8 | 7 | 6 | 5 | 4 | 3 | 2 | 1 | |
|----|----|----|----|----|----|---|---|---|---|---|---|---|---|---|---|
| | ◯ | | | | • | | | | • | | | | ◯ | | 7 |
| | | ◯ | | | • | ◯ | ∧ | ◯ | • | | | ◯ | | | 5 |
| | | | ◯ | | • | ◯ | ∧ | ◯ | • | | ◯ | | | | 3 |
| | | | | ◯ | • | ◯ | ∧ | ◯ | • | ◯ | | | | | 1 |

**Legend:**

| Symbol | Meaning | Symbol | Meaning |
|--------|---------|--------|---------|
| ☐ | Knit | ⋋ | sssk |
| • | Purl | ⋌ | k3tog |
| ◯ | Yo | ☐ | Pattern repeat |
| ∧ | sk2o | | |

## Dec Lace Pattern

| 21 | 20 | 19 | 18 | 17 | 16 | 15 | 14 | 13 | 12 | 11 | 10 | 9 | 8 | 7 | 6 | 5 | 4 | 3 | 2 | 1 | |
|----|----|----|----|----|----|----|----|----|----|----|----|---|---|---|---|---|---|---|---|---|---|
| | | ◯ | ⋌ | | | | • | | | | | • | | | ⋋ | ◯ | | | | | 7 |
| | ◯ | ⋌ | ◯ | ∧ | ◯ | | • | ◯ | ∧ | ◯ | • | | ◯ | ∧ | ◯ | ⋋ | ◯ | | | | 5 |
| ◯ | ⋌ | • | ◯ | ∧ | ◯ | | • | ◯ | ∧ | ◯ | • | | ◯ | ∧ | ◯ | • | ⋋ | ◯ | | | 3 |
| ◯ | ⋌ | • | ◯ | ∧ | ◯ | • | | ◯ | ∧ | ◯ | • | | ◯ | ∧ | ◯ | • | | ⋋ | ◯ | | 1 |

## Special instructions

### Inc Lace Pattern

**Row 1 (RS):** K1, yo, *p1, yo, sk2p, yo; rep from * to last 2 sts, p1, yo, k1.

**Rows 2, 4, 6 and 8 (WS):** K1, p to last st, k1.

**Row 3:** K1, yo, k1, *p1, yo, sk2p, yo; rep from * to last 3 sts, p1, k1, yo, k1.

**Row 5:** K1, yo, k2, *p1, yo, sk2p, yo; rep from * to last 4 sts, p1, k2, yo, k1.

**Row 7:** K1, yo, k3, *p1, k3; rep from * to last 5 sts, p1, k3, yo, k1.

### Dec Lace Pattern

**Row 1 (RS):** K1, yo, sssk, k1, *p1, yo, sk2p, yo; rep from * to last 6 sts, p1, k1, k3tog, yo, k1.

**Rows 2, 4, 6 and 8 (WS):** K1, p to last st, k1.

**Row 3:** K1, yo, sssk, *p1, yo, sk2p, yo; rep from * to last 5 sts, p1, k3tog, yo, k1.

**Row 5:** K1, yo, sssk, yo, sk2p, yo, *p1, yo, sk2p, yo; rep from * to last 4 sts, k3tog, yo, k1.

**Row 7:** K1, yo, sssk, k2, *p1, k3; rep from * to last 7 sts, p1, k2, k3tog, yo, k1.